BOB DYLAN HARMONICA

Arranged by Stephen Jennings

Stephen Jennings, compiler and arranger of this book, has been the editor of *Harmonica World* for the past seven years. In 1994, he received the Peter Jannsen Award from the International Harmonica Organisation for 'outstanding dedication in promoting interest in the harmonica'. Since studying harmonica with South Carolina blues legend Johnny Mars, Steve has appeared many times on radio and TV, and he makes regular appearances at gigs and festivals world wide.

Exclusive Distributors:
Hal Leonard
7777 West Bluemound Road,
Milwaukee, WI 53213
Email: info@halleonard.com
Hal Leonard Europe Limited
42 Wigmore Street, Marylebone,
London WIU 2 RY
Email: info@halleonardeurope.com
Hal Leonard Australia Pty. Ltd.
4 Lentara Court, Cheltenham,
Victoria 9132, Australia
Email: info@halleonard.com.au

Order No. AM932140
ISBN 0-7119-5196-9
This book © Copyright 1996 by Hal Leonard

Compiled and arranged by Stephen Jennings
Music processed by Interactive Sciences Limited
Book design by Pearce Marchbank, Studio Twenty
Cover photographs by London Features International

Printed in the EU.

More music books
For harmonica players...

Blues For Harmonica
28 tunes for both diatonic and chromatic harmonica, plus
extra seven pieces arranged for just chromatic
Instruments.
Order No. AM91948

The Rolling Stones For Harmonica
25 hit songs for both diatonic and chromatic harmonica
players with four more for just chromatic instruments.
Order No. AM91950

Jazz For Harmonica
27 great pieces for both diatonic and chromatic
harmonica players, plus 19 more for only chromatic
instruments.
Order No. AM91949

Rock For Harmonica
27 great pieces for both diatonic and chromatic
harmonica players, plus four more for only chromatic
instruments.
Order No.AM91946

The Beach Boys For Harmonica
16 hit songs for both diatonic and chromatic harmonica
players with eleven more for just chromatic instruments.
Order No. AM928500

Introduction

The arrangements in this book are aimed mainly at players of the ten hole major diatonic harmonica, or 'blues harp', although those tunes that would be beyond the technical reach of most players on the diatonic have been arranged for the twelve hole chromatic harmonica.

The tunes have been carefully selected and graded to provide something of interest for all players, from those who have recently started to play, and can play a few tunes and bend a couple of notes, to those who have a little more experience and are looking for melodic material upon which to try their skills.

The harmonica is well used as a solo instrument in the music of Bob Dylan, so as well as using these tunes as pieces of music in their own right, you should also use them to sharpen your improvisational skills — the chord sequences used in many of these songs can be very rewarding to play over.

It is often a good idea, and more fun than playing alone, to work on the pieces with a friend who plays guitar or keyboards to accompany you, or with one of the many programmable keyboards that are now available into which you have programmed the chords for the piece you are working on.

The Layout Of The Blues Harp

Below is a diagram showing all the notes available, both 'built-in' and obtainable by bending, on the ten hole major diatonic harmonica in the key of C, for which the tunes have been arranged.

The notes that are available by blowing or blow-bending are shown in capital letters, and those obtainable by drawing or draw-bending are shown in lower case letters.

Where more than one note is obtainable by bending, the note nearest the harmonica is that requiring the least amount of 'bend', and that furthest from the harmonica, the greatest.

Most of the draw bends appear some-where in this book, so it will be great bending practice for you, and a lot more interesting and enjoyable than just sitting playing exercises.

If you aren't sure if you're hitting quite the right note when bending, try playing the note you're trying to get on a keyboard, and then compare the sound with what you're getting from the harmonica.

Another idea is to use a chromatic electronic tuner, such as those used by guitarists, which will give you a very accurate indication as to how 'in tune' the bent notes are.

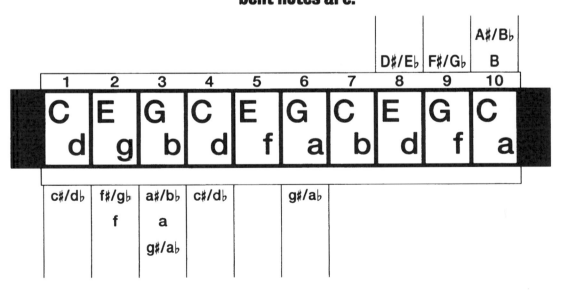

This may all sound a little daunting right now, but with a bit of practice and determination, you'll be playing those bends spot on all over the instrument, and wondering what all the fuss was about!

The Tablature

Here on this page is another representation of the information contained in the layout diagram, this time as musical notation and harmonica tablature. The names of the notes are given above them.

The tablature is easy to understand. A plain number means blow in that hole. A number in a circle means draw in that hole. The downward pointing arrowheads beneath encircled numbers mean bend the note in that hole by the number of steps indicated for. It is well worthwhile in the long run for you to gain some understanding of musical notation, so that you can read this information from the music, even if you are reading the actual notes from the tablature.

You will have noticed that in some places, two notes that look different and that have different names, are shown the same way in the tablature. This is due to the way that written music has developed in the Western world, and is known as enharmonic equivalence. What it boils down to is that,

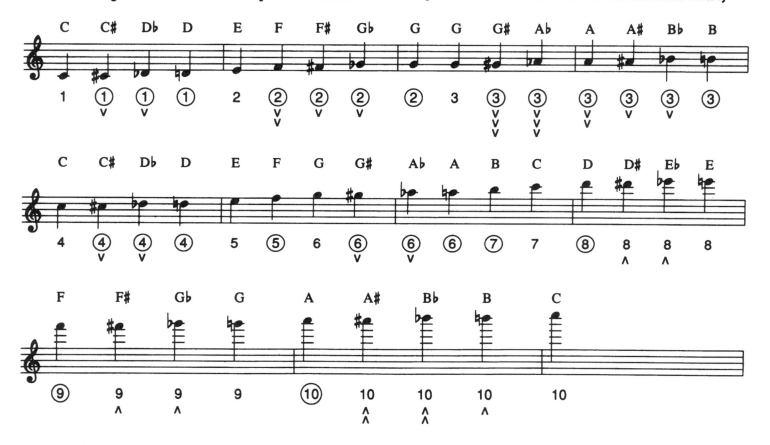

by the number of arrowheads. Each step is equal to a semitone.

Similarly, an upward pointing arrowhead beneath a blow note means blow bend that note by the number of steps indicated by the number of arrowheads.

On the C diatonic harmonica, the repeated G notes in draw 2 and blow 3 can be used interchangeably, at the discretion of the player. It is quite possible that in the music in this book, you will prefer to use blow 3 in places where draw 2 is indicated, and vice versa. This is entirely a matter of personal taste, there is no single right way of going about it. Do what feels most natural and comfortable to you.

One of the drawbacks of tablature like this is that while it can tell you what notes to play, it cannot tell you how long to play them

depending on the circumstances, every note may be called one of several things. You will see that on the C harmonica, this applies to the bent notes, which coincide with the black notes on a keyboard, which are by far the most common targets for this dual naming convention.

The tablature for the chromatic harmonica is even simpler. Blow and draw notes are shown as for the diatonic — a plain number means blow that hole, an encircled number means draw that hole. A leftward pointing arrow beneath either a blow or a draw note means depress the slide button, and blow or draw as appropriate.

There are many more duplicated notes on the chromatic than on the diatonic, and again, which you use is a matter of personal taste and style of playing. The patterns given are designed to give the smoothest possible way through each tune.

If, however, you have difficulty with them, remember that draw 2, button out and blow 2, button in, give the same note, F— the same applies to draw 6, button out and blow 6, button in and draw 10, button out and blow 10, button in. Blow 4, button out, blow 5, button out and draw 4, button in, give the same note, C—the same applies to blow 8, button out, blow 9, button out and draw 8, button in. Blow 4, button in and blow 5, button in give the same note, C# — the same applies to blow 8, button in and blow 9, button in. So you may be able to find an alternative route through the piece that you find more comfortable to play.

Chromatic players who are able to read music are encouraged to try the pieces that have been arranged for the diatonic —they will sound just as good on either instrument. Please note that in places where double sharps or double flats should, according to strict musical theory, appear, their enharmonic equivalent natural notes have been used in order to make using the book easier.

Above all, have fun!

Further Information
...about reading music can be found in
'How To Read Music' by Helen Cooper
Order No. OP41904 (book only); AM91452 (Book and matching CD)
...about the diatonic harmonica, including bending notes and the physics of how bending works can be found in
'The Harp Handbook' by Steve Baker
Order No. BWH7219 (book only); BRM7219 (Matching CD)
...about basic bending techniques can be found in
'Bending The Blues' by David Harp
Order No.DH10054

ALL ALONG THE WATCHTOWER

Words & Music by Bob Dylan

Moderately, with a beat

BLOWIN' IN THE WIND

Words & Music by Bob Dylan

Moderately bright

GOTTA SERVE SOMEBODY

Words & Music by Bob Dylan

Moderately slow

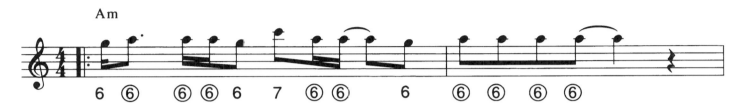

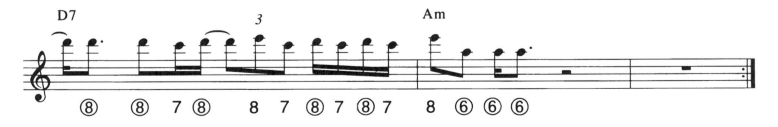

IDIOT WIND

Words & Music by Bob Dylan

Slowly, with a steady beat

11

Shelter From The Storm

Words & Music by Bob Dylan

Moderately

SHOT OF LOVE

Words & Music by Bob Dylan

Moderately slow

SAD EYED LADY OF THE LOWLANDS

Words & Music by Bob Dylan

Moderately slow

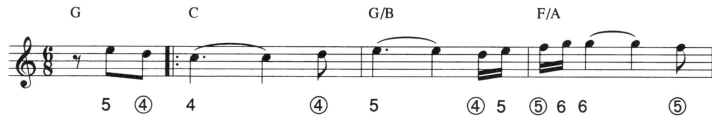

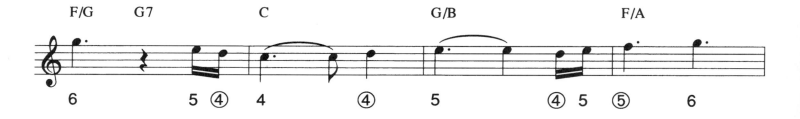

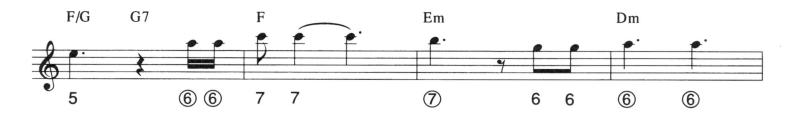

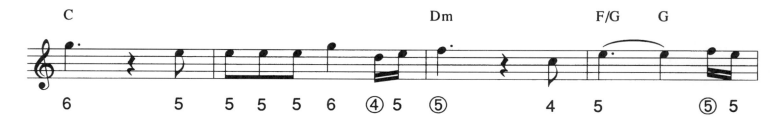

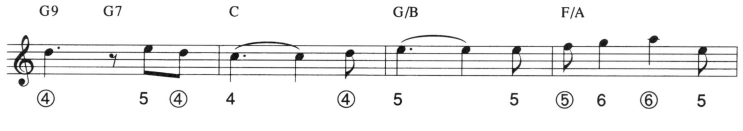

I WANT YOU

Words & Music by Bob Dylan

Moderately bright

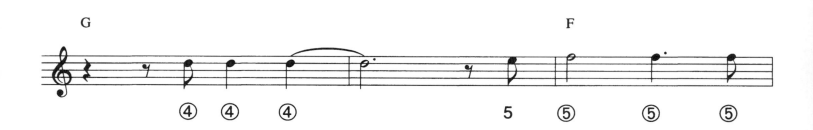

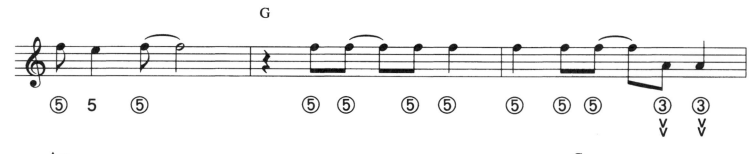

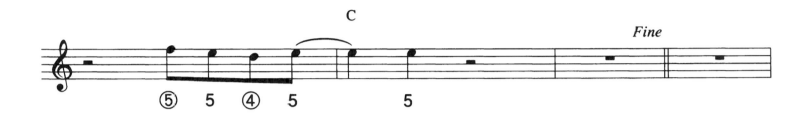

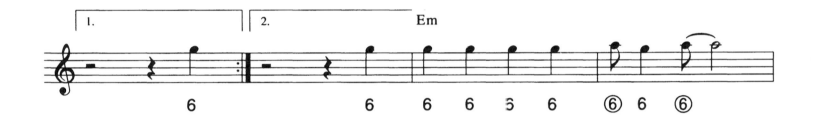

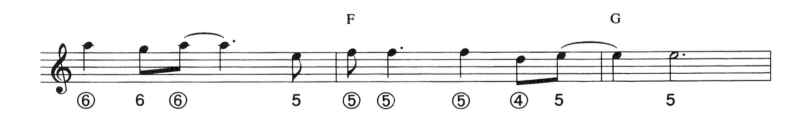

IS YOUR LOVE IN VAIN?

Words & Music by Bob Dylan

Moderately slow

IF NOT FOR YOU

Words & Music by Bob Dylan

Moderately bright

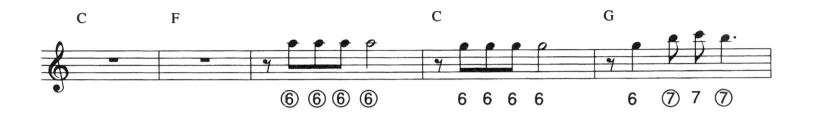

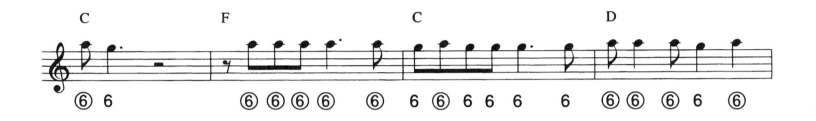

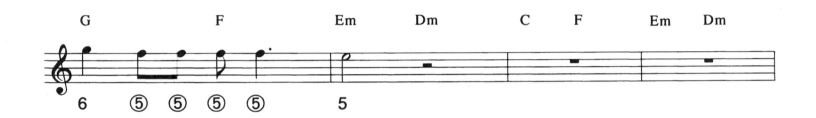

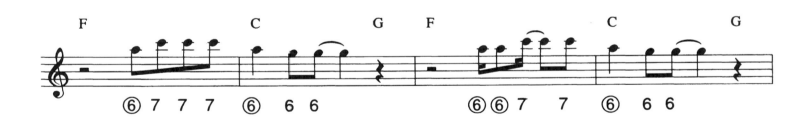

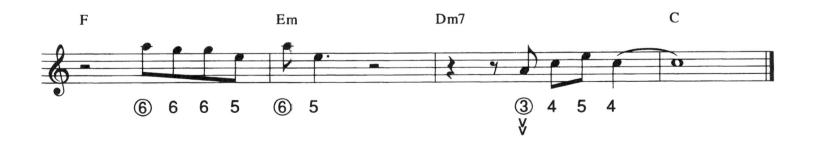

SOMETHING THERE IS ABOUT YOU

Words & Music by Bob Dylan

Moderately bright

SHENANDOAH

Traditional. Arranged by Bob Dylan

Moderately

STUCK INSIDE OF MOBILE WITH THE MEMPHIS BLUES AGAIN

Words & Music by Bob Dylan

I SHALL BE RELEASED

Words & Music by Bob Dylan & Richard Manuel

JOKERMAN

Words & Music by Bob Dylan

SIMPLE TWIST OF FATE

Words & Music by Bob Dylan

Moderately

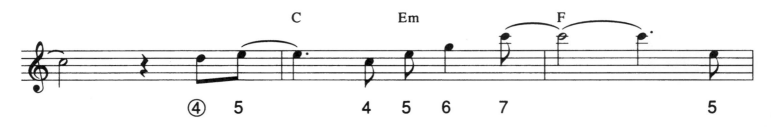

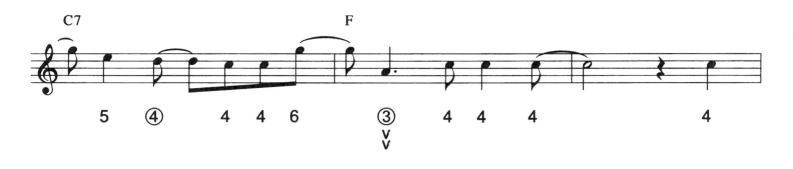

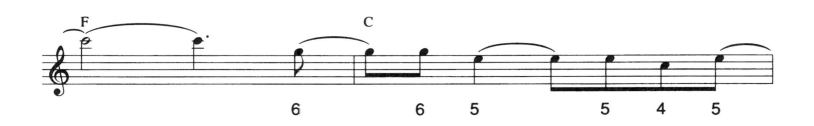

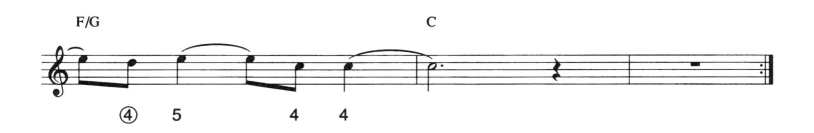

BROWNSVILLE GIRL

Words & Music by Bob Dylan & Sam Sheppard

Slowly

LAY, LADY, LAY

Words & Music by Bob Dylan

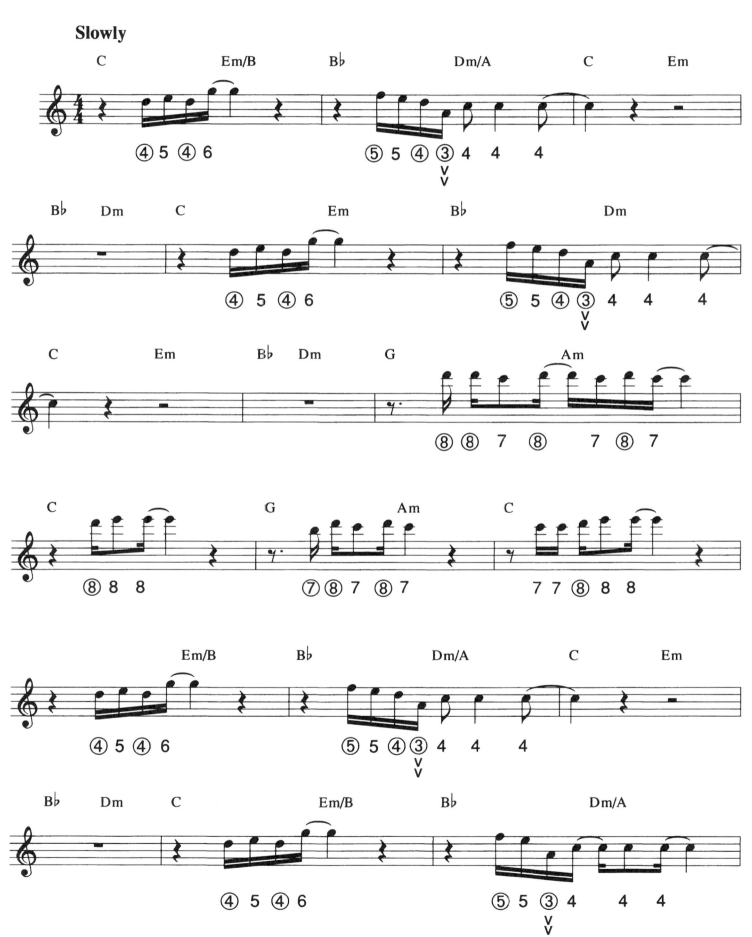

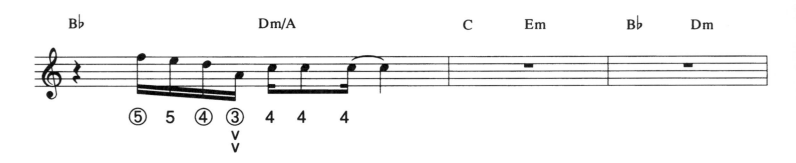

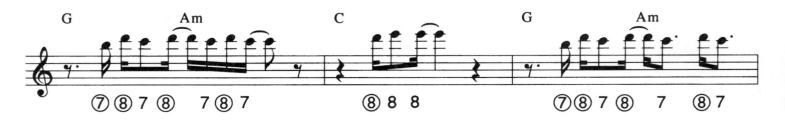

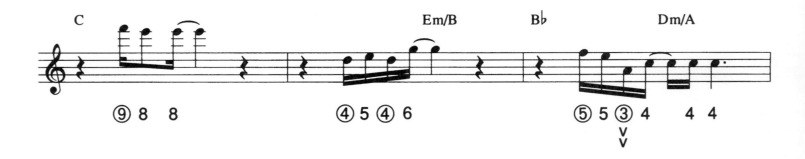

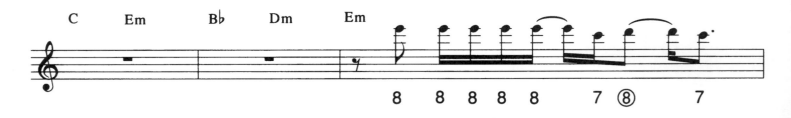

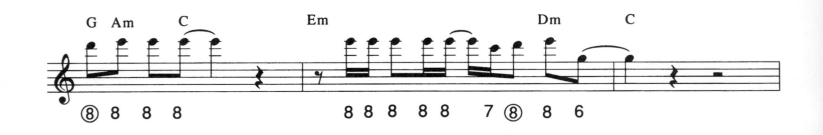

KNOCKIN' ON HEAVEN'S DOOR

Words & Music by Bob Dylan

HURRICANE

Music by Bob Dylan

Words by Bob Dylan & Jacques Levy

TANGLED UP IN BLUE

Words & Music by Bob Dylan

Moderately

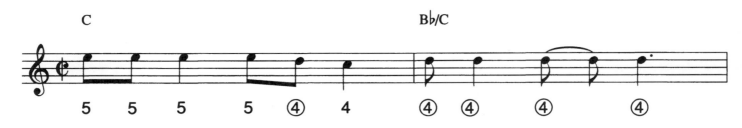

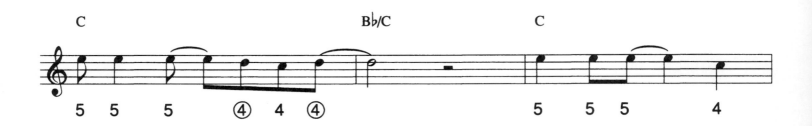

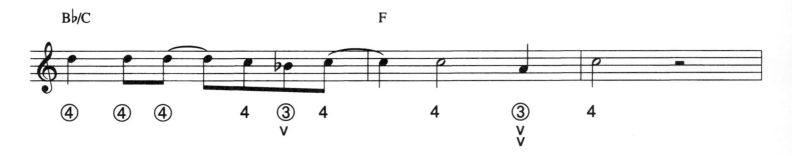

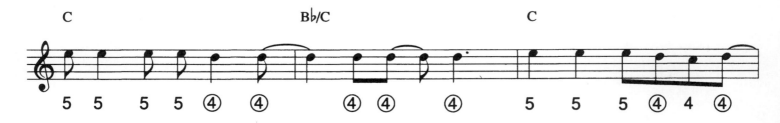

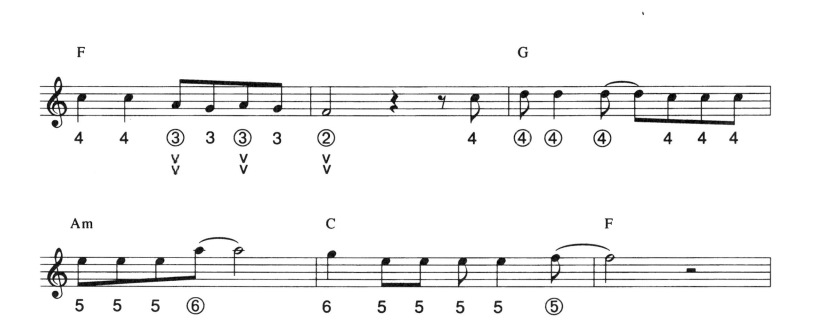

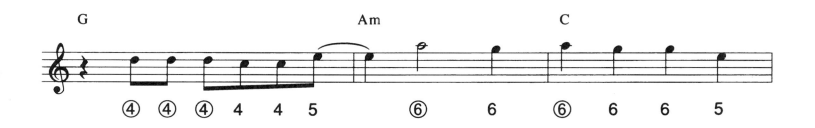

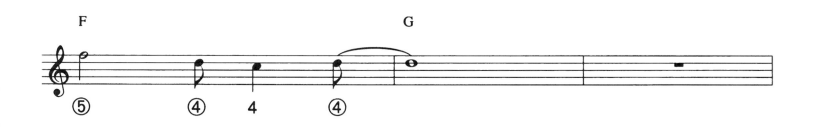

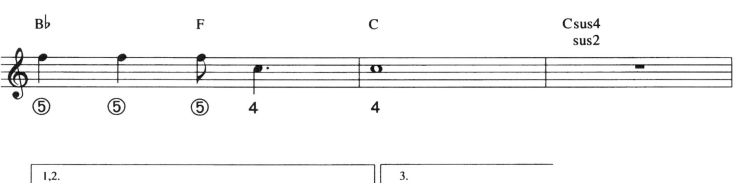

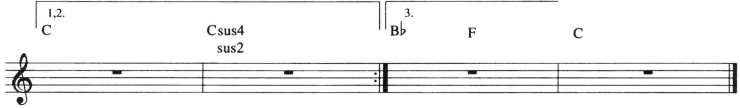

JUST LIKE A WOMAN

Words & Music by Bob Dylan

Moderately slow

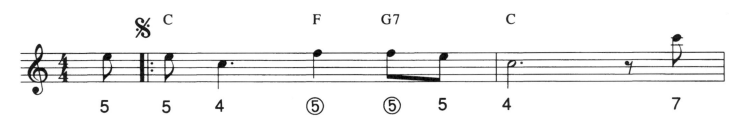

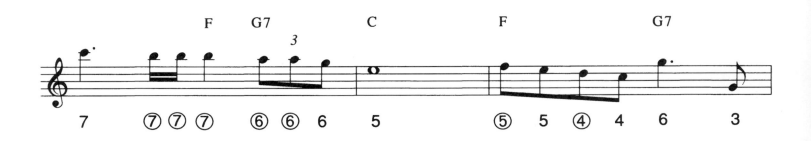

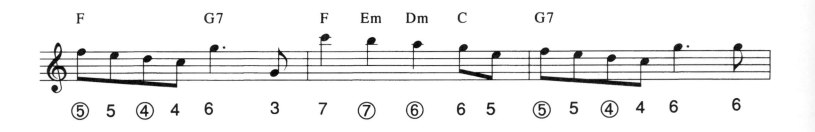

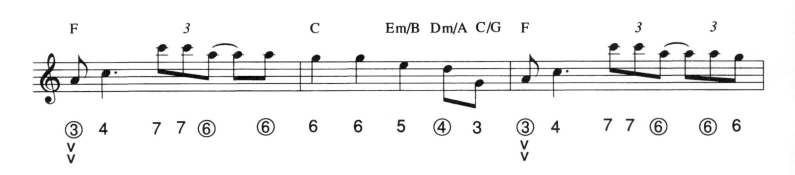

SARA

Words & Music by Bob Dylan

Moderately

QUINN THE ESKIMO (THE MIGHTY QUINN)

Words & Music by Bob Dylan

Moderately slow, with a beat

IN THE GARDEN

Words & Music by Bob Dylan

Moderately slow

I'LL BE YOUR BABY TONIGHT

Words & Music by Bob Dylan

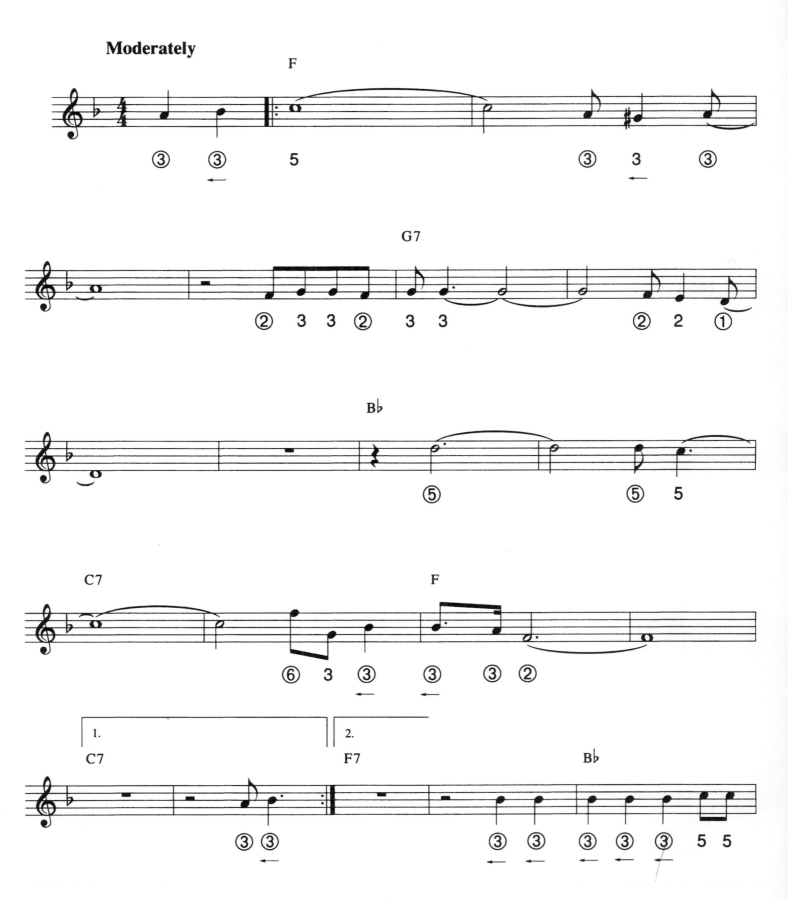

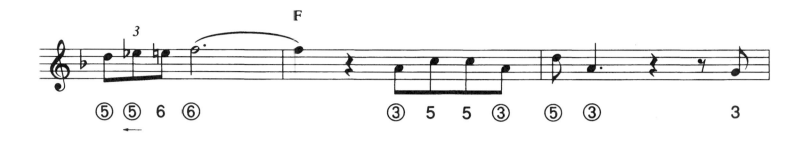

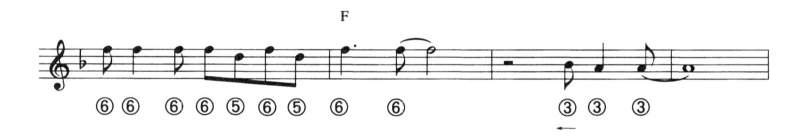

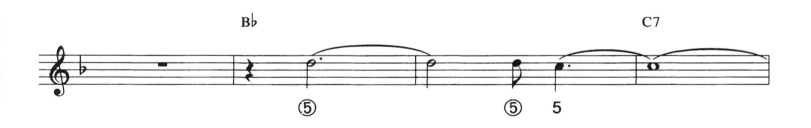

EVERYTHING IS BROKEN

Words & Music by Bob Dylan

Moderately

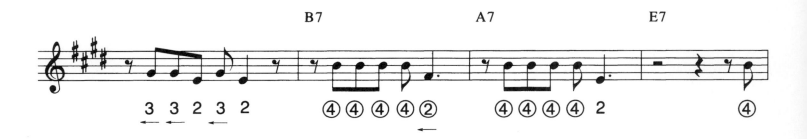

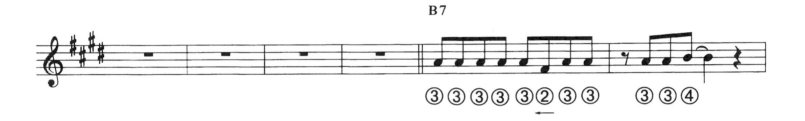

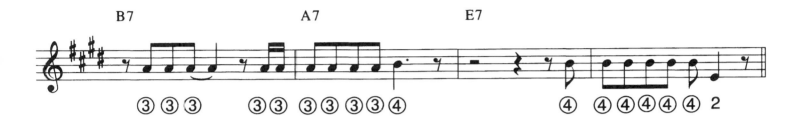

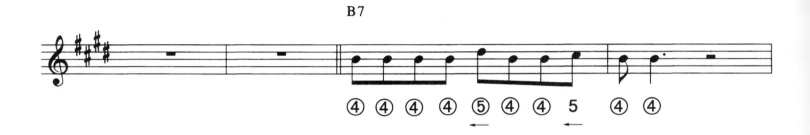

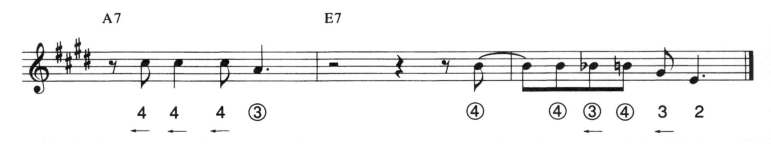

RAINY DAY WOMEN Nos 12 & 35

Words & Music by Bob Dylan

UNDER YOUR SPELL

Words & Music by Bob Dylan & Carole Bayer Sager

Moderately slow

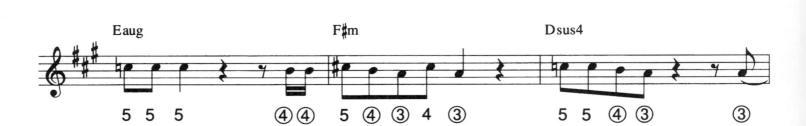

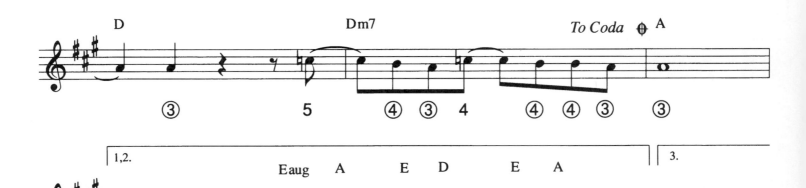

SILVIO

Words & Music by Bob Dylan & Robert Hunter

Moderately bright

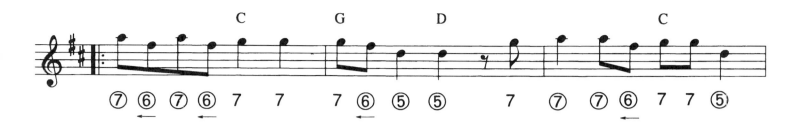

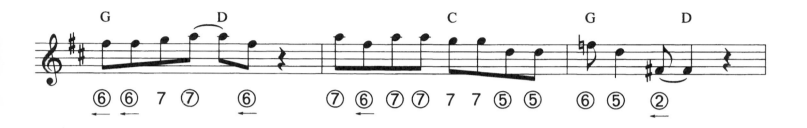

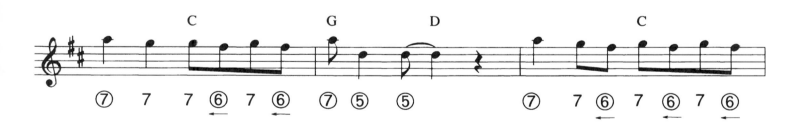